CONTENTS

INTRODUCTION

PERSONALIA

In Memory of My Father
Personal History
Post Booby-trap
Foreign Visitors
Masks
Encounter
Announcement
Sea-shell
The Dream
Dancing the Dusk
Self-Righteous
Privileged
Read from the Altar

QUIET PATHWAYS

Quest
Carrickbracken
Caldragh Statue
Famine
Observation
The Master's Tally
Winter Tryst
The Removal
Mountain Evening
The *Clochán* Speaks
Specification

SET TIMES

Spring Sowing
May-fire
Midsummer Pilgrimage
Cutting the *Cailleach*
Autumn Gypsy
All Soul's Night
The Christmas

SONNETS ON A SPECKLED STONE

On Cemetery Sunday
Newry Market Recovered
Swallows at Carrickbracken
Summer Idyll
Benburb Priory

RANDOM GATHERINGS

Presents
Passion-tide
The Sacrament of the Scarf
A Merchant Prince
Mucky *Pieta*
Welcome the Singer
Imagination
Vendor
European Union
Love Song
Lucy
Pickpocket
Trout
Pilgrims

INTRODUCTION

It is a cool morning in October as I open my door to admit the day into this quiet home of mine.

My house, its rough grey face weather-carved, yet pulsating with life, occupies a half-hidden hollow among the little hills that climb ever upwards towards the bulk of the purple mountain which rises behind us, and which in turn serves as a footstool for great Slieve Gullion that rears its crest among the craggy mountains just beyond.

The front door opens on to a yard - called *the street* in this locality. My street faces northwards, and serves as a platform from which to view events of significance - a blazing sunset perhaps, or the clouds of rooks which wheel around the venerable Church Rock tower over yonder, bickering noisily among themselves before they settle for the night. And once, on a morning such as this, I watched a pair of swans, pewter flames in the half-light, winging their way up to the neighbouring lake, and leaving in their wake the echoing lament of their passing. Here too I stood as a boy upon a brilliantly starlit night to gaze awestruck, and not a little frightened, at a comet that was passing in profound silence through the frigid infinity of the heavens. And somehow at that moment, or certainly around that time, my soul-child caught consciousness, and this countryside became templified into sacred space for me.

For this is an ancient landscape, and there, stretched out before me like a net straining to catch the meaning-music of the placenames, whose origins are lost in history, is the warp-and-weft of the surrounding townlands: Cross, Divernagh, Carrivekeeny, Maghernahely, Carrickcloghan; and closer to hand, there is Carrickcruppen, the gravestones of whose cemetery I can sometimes see glimmering mysteriously through the trees, and where the remains of so many generations of the parish lie buried.

And, as these placenames would indicate, once upon a day, and indeed until not so long ago, Irish, which would link us with deep antiquity indeed, was the commonly used language. Now it has all but melted away, like snow off a ditch, although courageous efforts are currently being made to revive it....

Even a mere generation ago the variety of English spoken here featured many words of Irish, and some of the physical features of the landscape echoed Gaelic names - names like *Páirc-a-tobair*, the well-field; and the *Brocar*, or field of badgers....

In some way in all this, I am reminded of Robin Flower the noted English-born Celtic scholar, who spent much time living among the people of the Blasket Islands off the Kerry coast.

In his book, "The Irish Tradition"' Flower, describes how he "...was wandering idly one day along a road upon an island three miles out into the Atlantic beyond the most westerly point of Ireland." As he walked, Flower encountered an old man digging potatoes in a field and the two fell into conversation. Flower describes how, during their conversation, the old man began to recite from memory lengthy passages from ancient and generally long-forgotten Gaelic poems and tales, and he continues: "....I listened spellbound and, as I listened, it came to me suddenly that....I was hearing the oldest living tradition in the British Isles.... Tomorrow this too will be dead, and the world will be poorer when this last shade of that which once was great has passed away."

★ ★ ★ ★

Just down the road is the Glen, a deep gash in the earth that was perhaps formed by some cataclysmic upheaval when all the world was young. Only a few hundred yards in length, and with steeply sloping sides, the atmosphere here is one of mystery. The Glen is home to a small forest of beeches, whose autumn foliage of golden-leaf, even on the most overcast of days, turns the dark valley into a brightly glowing crucible.

However, beneath the beechen canopy the light is subdued enough, filtering down, as it does, in hazy streamers through the uppermost branches and rendering the wood reminiscent of a church interior, with the great grey tree trunks as pillars; for although bird-song is perfectly audible here, the overall spirit of the place is one of stillness.

Along the western-most lip of the valley meanders a tiny stream of clear water in its bed of golden sand, and whose chuckling music provides contrast to the cloak of solemnity which seems to enwrap us here....

But soon now we will fare forth-a-walking, you and I. But no ordinary walk this, no mere prosaic stroll between the fences of the everyday, but a pilgrimage to the hidden places of soul, where paradox dwells and where the prosaically rational awaits to be transformed into something quite different....

And so let our path lead upwards....

PERSONALIA

5

In Memory of my Father
- *a celebration* –

Off-white in thick curdles
Hawthorn blooms dripped
Clotted-cream-like and
Swayed upon the hedges
Of McCourt's field.
May it was, dusk and
Dream-time silent as
Hand-in-hand we strolled
Through the massing hay,
My father's shining brown
Shoes dusting into gold
With pollen, his hair a
Silver filigree.
He stopped, and turning to me
Asked: *Won't you remember*
This evening for me always, Brian?
In eight year old solemnity I
Gave my word.
To-day, my father, in a song
I have kept my promise,
For angelic to me were you then,
But today, God-like.

Personal History

I am of Ulster, where born among my father's
Catholic clan in Down, I early learned the values
Of our Presbyterian neighbours - thrift, hard
Work, and keep the place looking Protestant. On
The other hand, half my personal history is
Scribed across the stern face of a small South-
Armagh farm, where every field, laboriously
Ground by my maternal ancestors from the harsh
Granite of life's mountain is a white page that
Today is furrowed by lines of rich dark print.
Along these electric rows of energy live words
Cavort, a fecund crop, with every word a green
Plant and it to be wringing wet, all salty and
Damp and sappy with meaning. Yet for us, my
Friend, since you and I are separate folk, each
Word will tell a slightly different tale. Therefore
Read carefully between the lines, for often enough
It's in the holiness of that strange sanctuary of the
Betwixt and the between where visceral profundities
Of truth will flourish most, to be perceived and
Tasted only by those perversely blind enough to see.

Post Booby-Trap

Across the bloated meadow in the rain-shine
I watched a row of stooping troopers go
-As quiet garments bobbing on a clothesline
In the savage evening glow.

They seemed a row of gleaning harvesters,
Each man's harvest-bag a-bulge with grain.
But the crop they garnered was a flesh one-
Lacerated parts-that-make-a man, and bits of brain.

Then in the denseness of the dripping overhead
The helicopters whined like maddened flies -
An elegy for all the helpless loved ones
Slain on the altar of an Irish sacrifice.

Foreign Visitors

Beneath the bleak tombstone of a January sky

We wrestled all day to splice our snipped fence,

Angrily securing loose posts with sledge-slugged

Blows until the gluey earth resounded with

Vibrating thuds. Then barbed-wire serpents bucked

In glinting coils to rip bloody scores in numb

Hands as lengths were measured off between the crazy

Uprights. Afterwards we garrotted the slack to

Tautness and smashed home fastening staples

In the dozy wood. Five strands in all there

Were, a kind of staff to sound in minor mode

The music of our threatened dispossession.

Masks
- Travelling on the Larne-Stranraer Ferry -

Loudmouthed and boisterous
As school-boys out of uniform the
Home-going unit entered the lounge,
Close-cropped and warily lean as
Criminals. But I in their midst
Pretended absorption in the *Irish News*,
Aware I too was branded alien.
One sat beside me, and I at once
Remembering the ancestral defilement
Of my land and people dutifully recoiled.
Then he offered me a cigarette,
And as if for the first time I saw a
Lad from a Galloway farm, a chapter
Of our tormented Ulster story agonised and
Writhing in his childish eyes. We smoked
Together and painfully I read how he
Laughed with assumed bravado at my suggestion
Of his terror under sniper fire on a
Belfast street patrol. Now sometimes I
Feel a great lonesomeness for I know that
In that single splinter of eternity I'd met
A boy who could have been my son.

PERSONALIA

Encounter

In memory of Frank Kerr,
my kinsman and friend,
who died on 10 November 1994

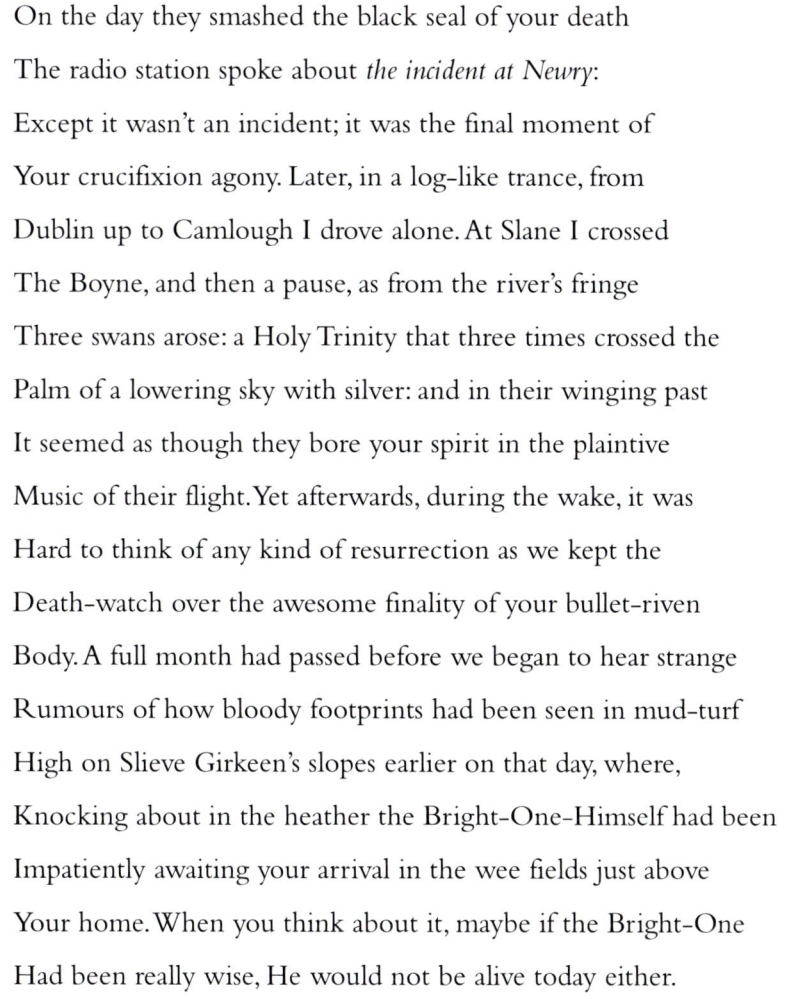

On the day they smashed the black seal of your death

The radio station spoke about *the incident at Newry*:

Except it wasn't an incident; it was the final moment of

Your crucifixion agony. Later, in a log-like trance, from

Dublin up to Camlough I drove alone. At Slane I crossed

The Boyne, and then a pause, as from the river's fringe

Three swans arose: a Holy Trinity that three times crossed the

Palm of a lowering sky with silver: and in their winging past

It seemed as though they bore your spirit in the plaintive

Music of their flight. Yet afterwards, during the wake, it was

Hard to think of any kind of resurrection as we kept the

Death-watch over the awesome finality of your bullet-riven

Body. A full month had passed before we began to hear strange

Rumours of how bloody footprints had been seen in mud-turf

High on Slieve Girkeen's slopes earlier on that day, where,

Knocking about in the heather the Bright-One-Himself had been

Impatiently awaiting your arrival in the wee fields just above

Your home. When you think about it, maybe if the Bright-One

Had been really wise, He would not be alive today either.

Announcement

Great Creator of the fertile darkness, it is I who would
Repent for not having right joyfully run before your holy
Tide: it's too content I've been to dutifully ply the ponds
Of stagnant life, propelled by the sterile breeze of
Others' counsel. But now, for a short time only

Can I hold this course, for lively, the strong
Current that gushes beneath my keel, would twist
The rudder, slipping my delicate curragh from out the
Dull roads of all that is conventional and turning my
Prow towards the fearsomeness of waters unfamiliar.

You alone, oh great Christ of greenness, know whither I
Am bound: no longer can I ignore the prodigality of moist
Ecstasy that cascades over me from the pool of heaven,
And bitter indeed is my sorrow that for so long did I
Regard it as fitting matter for my confessional whisper.

PERSONALIA

Sea-shell

Minutely convex, and breast-like feminine on the
Dry bank of my desk-top rests the limpet-shell you

Carried from Iona. Her surface lucent-bronzed,
The channelled flutes are grooved, delicate,

Delicate as runnels for spilled milk's flow: within
Her satined cusp, the scallop-edge brimmed with

Brass-like braid, I see the image of your face
That right lovingly smiles at me as out the dim

Recesses of a bonnet's shade. And from my
Shell's depths, as though by bell's tongue tolled,

It seems that I discern the rhythmic tides of sea's
Thud upon Iona's beach, and veining through

The chanting of her ghostly monks, that voice of yours,
Which always seems to sing a blessing on my world.

The Dream

Once upon a night of ragged
Dreams, and before you really knew
Me, across the barren reaches of
The soul you called my name. And
Then you came, all radiant in
Plaid and apple-green: about your

Neck a string of pearls - each one
A clouded moonlet. But somewhere
In the muddied darkness of my
Story I'd lost the music of my
Heart. You said: *Through hearing
Mine you'll hear again your own.*

And so, against your breast you drew
My head, and then it was I listened
To the harmony that healed,
For through the singing of your heart
I clearly heard an echo of
The music that belonged to me.

Dancing the Dusk

Once, between the lights I saw
You dance. Beside the hazel grove
It was, whose little trees stretched
Up to paint the very brightness of
The dusk of June. Oh you have
Danced too where fall cascades
Of quiet light, where foxgloves wave,
And flowering hawthorns charge
The twilit air with beauty. And I have
Seen the circle of your reel that flickered
Faint among the quivering rowans
Of the speedwelled banks that cast
The spangles of their dappled
Shadows on the surface of the lake.
Dance on lone Dancer of the edge
Of dark, for there is music in your eyes
And tiny rainbows plait your hair in glories.

Self-righteous

The force of his knocking reverberated
About my door in irritable brazenness,
And on my answering the door
I found there a tramp,

Stinking clothes like ripped sails
Slung from some shipwrecked
Yardarm. Most foul he was with dead
Drink, sweat and a hell-full

Of nameless sins, the front of
His trousers dank and
Reeking of spilt urine. He demanded
Tea, and when I gave it

He reached out and grasped
My hand in gratitude. Afterwards
I went in to purge the stench
Of him, and as I washed my hands

In scented toilet soap I had
The grace to feel like Pilate, who
Having sat in judgment,
Once sent Truth a-gurgling down
The whirling outlet of a sink.

Privileged

*Stay by the books, Son: they'll not let you down... The
Education's easy carried... No place here
For the likes of you without it...* Mantras of
My Northern boyhood, and I to mind a drizzly

Summer dusk in a country ceili-house,
Watching, as silent men sloped shyly in for
Evening fix of company and strong tobacco –
Unshaven, field-labouring men, who gruffed in

Painful monosyllable of politics
And prices, and freely spat upon the
Concrete floor... To clinch some argument
About a coming cattle-fair, old James as

Master-of-the-House arose, and from the
Dusky archive of his mantel-piece drew down
A copy of *Old Moore's Almanac* and, with
A flourish, handed it to me. Then turning to

His audience announced *We've got a scholar
Here the-night, one of our own!* And opening
The soot-stained text, he bade me read aloud
That all might hear. In that brusque request I

Realised that for those men I wore the mantle
Of their envoy to the land of schools returned
To rest a while among my people in the
Curlew-ringing fastness of an Ulster bog.

PERSONALIA

Read from the Altar

Introibo ad altare Dei. Ad Deum qui laetificat juventutem meum…
Psalm 42:4
And I will go in to the altar of God : to God who giveth joy to my youth…
Douay-Rheims 1899 American Edition (DRA)

Lent was once a green iceberg, and I an altar-boy,
Which placed me well within the fold, although in surplice
And red soutane I could have seemed a down-sized cardinal
….And I am nine years old again, serving Mass upon
A Lenten Sunday, crocus-spiked and crystalline, the
Chapel aromatic with stale incense smoke and
Burning candle-wax, and my fingers frigid from
Preparing cruets on the marble credence
Table: one glass goblet is pure with water, the
Other dark with the languid muskiness of
Sacrificial wine….Then Mass begins, and as the
Solemn rite requires, I mount the altar steps to
Shift (in my uncertain way) the brazen bookstand
Together with its massive missal. But as I, right
Shakily, descend again the steps, my foot becomes
Enclogged within the cassock's fold, and I fall down, the
Lectern crashing madly on the sanctuary
Floor and the pages of the holy Book forlornly
Fluttering in what seems a sad reproach. And in
My confusion, as I attempt to gather up
My burden of defilement, I vaguely hear the
Angry priest condemn me for a fool before
The sanctity of that Sabbath-silent multitude.

PERSONALIA

QUIET PATHWAYS

19

Quest

In my grandfather's house I listened
To old men passing the hour,
And they told me how high on the mountain
I once owned a magic flower –
That blazed in the blood-red heather,
Putting the winds to shame
Like a badge on a royal bosom
Awaiting a monarch's claim.

Then I swore that I'd be the lover
Who would cull that bloom for my bride,
So I fashioned scissors of music
And went out on the mountain-side,
But the land was a purple dreamscape
Enclosed in sunshine bars
Where the sward lay green beneath me
And the marigolds all were stars.

Through the empty fields I have wandered
In search of my fleeting prize,
Though the depths of the hills have whispered
That it's not for human eyes.
Yet still must I go questing
Through Carrickbracken and Cross
For that flower in the haunted heather
To assuage my aching loss.

Carrickbracken

-For Kathleen who died many years ago-

When Kathleen went to milk the cow
The byre began to tune and ring.
It had become a violin –
God's finger plying on the string.

The townland sang in harmony
With gently pulsing sigh.
The evening had become a church,
And the Holy Ghost was passing by.

Caldragh Statue

Trickster of the half-light, tricky in the dawn
The waters of Lough Erne skipping jump and beam,
Holding in enchantment the notes of darkness dying,
Blinking in the wonder of the fresh sun's gleam.

And out in Boa Island, tranquil swans awake
To watch the moon dissolve in a pinkly-purple sky.
The day is fast unwrapping and melody is gracing,
As thrush-song mingles with a lake-bird's cry.

In the lonely graveyard calm the statue stands there,
With bearded Janus faces and eyes that widely stare.
They seem to slit the membrane 'twixt now and the eternal
In this soporific dell with its hawthorn scented air.

About the timeless image skeins of mystery ravel,
And spells that mystic island-seers have incensed in a haze
Twine the stillness of the watchers with their tendrils of magic,
As they wait entranced forever lost in hypnotising gaze.

Caldragh Statue:
Situated in Boa Island, which lies in Lower Lough Erne in County Fermanagh, is Caldragh cemetery. This tiny, almost hidden, enclosure is surrounded by brushwood rather than trees, and has the atmosphere of the traditional Gaelic tearmann, or sanctuary. In the centre of the burial ground stand the mysterious Caldragh statues, the larger of the two being the more compelling. Possessed of two pointed faces looking in opposite directions and standing about two feet high, it is thought that this Janus-faced artifact may have been fashioned and placed here after the arrival of Christianity, but it is not known whether or not it is purely pagan in origin.

Famine

Thank God for the new priddies. There'll be no hunger the year now.
Traditional Prayer spoken as the first bucket of new potatoes was brought in.
MICHAEL J. MURPHY *At Slieve Gullion's Foot.*

Somewhere in a bleak niche of my grandfather's memory
There must have hung a glass, in which he perhaps saw
Mirrored a mother pregnant with death, and whose affair
With hunger had goaded her to stand upon his father's
Street in shivering humility. Begging a mug of yellow meal

She was: enough to carry her to the Newry boat and onward.
Today I wonder did his stomach turn with vestigial drift of
The famine-fever taint, when once, with Mosaic indignation
He rebuked me, having seen me cast upon the fire potato
Scraps remaining from a family meal. Mayhap too on that

Day he listened to some primal stirring of a famine dirge
Lamenting other days that rose to blight a hopeful harvest-time:
A Dhia na ngrást, tá dubh ar na préataí arís.[1]
And did he somehow feel the peaceful eccentricity of a land where
Birdsong played amid the guardian hedges of the leprous fields?

---

[1] **God of graces, the blight is on the potatoes again!**

Observation

…they also observe the ritual of a churning, a weekly
Alchemy which entails the rhythmic thrust of a
Sun-headed staff deep into the wooden womb of
A churn. Plunging thus through the leaden clouts
Of thickened cream within, they pray the god of
Resurrection that in the chaotic universe of the milky
Nebula they create, a can of stars will birth. Quite
Suddenly it seems to happen: for a shoal of butter-bright
Flakes bursts, golden sprat-like exploding in a deckled
Mosaic on the face of the pierced disc. And it's then
Their coarse-tiled scullery floor becomes a temple stage,
Where Ordinary dances madrigal with Miracle…Once,
When waking suddenly from habitual sleep, I thought
I glimpsed the fleeting shadow of Divinity smile in at
Them from the silent sun-filled basin of the empty street…

The Master's Tally

In memory of Michael McParland, National Teacher

A harsh man! the parish wiseacres cried, before they forgot
Me, for I stood aloof from earthy ways. And yet, in
Their midst, just atop yon brae, and somewhere in that

Nettle-jungled spillage of years there stood my home,
Where now a single jutting rib of tarred-roof fragment rises
To point an accusatory finger. Here, unknown to all I once

Enticed a bride, who, having sung her song for me, sang no more,
But fled a single summer after into bluer skies. She couldn't
Bear schoolmasterish ways she said. Then it was that with

The lonely consolation of my books I wrought throughout
The night to calibrate love's mystery in terms of icy calculus:
To capture all its pain and glory within the curving arches of

A graph, and sought to con its story in the crabbed pages of the
Greek. Only when the dawn made mockery of my quivering
Lamp-flame did my lessons speak to me. *The pears of life are*

Not for Augustinian plundering, but the Golden Apples may
Yet be plucked. Afterwards, when I died, I bequeathed my
Everything to Nuns for the education of a girl-child.

Winter Tryst

Graceful indeed as the flight of a white swan above
The Curved Lake is the walk of you, or as the
Arching flash of the choice salmon splashing

Silver on the smooth lip of a frozen weir.
Sweet-scented you are too, your odour rich as
The smell of the winter bracken that blows from the

Bare ridge of Slieve Gullion, or clean as the blade
Of the east wind that would be sweeping out of
The cloud that cloaks the wee hills. But it is I who

Would come gladly to you at noon, or at that
Time between the lights, or through the depths
Of the darkness itself, if you would but beckon:

And before the ruddiness of your bright fire
We'd sit, the two of us together, not shyly at all,
Forever sheltered against the black storms of the

World. For wouldn't it be to the Monarch of
High glory that the warm passion of our love would
Pour, and it as a sweet hymn of everlasting praise.

The Removal

-In memory of Dark Moninna, once a weaver of damask-

On the kitchen mantelpiece the stopped alarm clock
Was the prosaic nebula that births eternity.
Ach, well God have mercy on her soul,
A man arriving muttered gruffly.

Then later that evening, just before
We lifted, a sort of resonant dullness
Like a grey fleece, enwrapped the wake, and
Gradually the bustle braked as reluctant,

Half-shyly almost, we gathered subdued,
Buttressing each other to courage in
The curtained room that church-like
Smelt of melted candle-wax and autumn

Flowers. Across from the linen-masked
Mirror of a sideboard, the lidless coffin
Lay on silver trestles. It was awkwardly
Self-conscious each of us was to face

Finally the shrouded dignity of its gentle tenant,
Her almost ninety years of growing graciousness
Dissonant with the harshness of her going:
Too well her death had plumbed the tarn-depth

Fear of all our passings and peeled away
The banal from the palimpsest of our lives.
I gave the Rosary out, and then, the
Coffin closed, we carried her in fours to

Chapel, our arms as comrades' wound
About each other's shoulders. Behind
Us walked our neighbours and through
The shimmering aurora of their muted chat

Of crops and stock and other clayey things
I sensed the spirit that lightly danced
Along with us caress us, each one gently,
In the August stillness of a Camlough lane.

Mountain Evening

In memory of Michael O'Hagan, Gentleman

Surely God keeps an unruly classroom the times she teaches in the
University of the heart, with Slieve Girkeen alight with foxgloves, and
Dew-fall as her rostrum. For I remember a lecture, soul-slitting as
Larksong, that she once read to a class of listening sycamores and
I eavesdropping from a dusk-washed bank of an evening, when the
Mountain was Tabor and the form that was in the smoke of the burning
Whins that Micky was sending up from behind a heathery
Shoulder was the seething shape of cosmic Transfiguration. Blue-grey
Then the path, and tar-crocheted black after the heat of June: a river
It would seem, draining the barrel of time's reservoir away to
Endlessness down the fall of the hillside between the hemlock's lacy
Cuffs that ruffled the dim wrists of the twilight. But there, deep in the
Sombre valley there'd always be shining the blade of the curved lake,
Ever a faithful rent of quiet brightness in the frayed hem of Christ's day,
And it pledging to the coming night the promise of a tranquil afterwards.

The *Clochán* Speaks

-A verse for Genevieve's guest-book-

I stand beside the busy way
That from the heathered summit spills
To Kevin's valley, pilgrim-grey,
Enwrapped among the quiet hills.

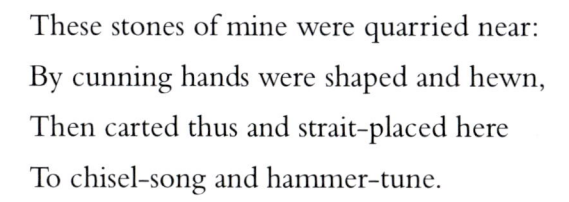

These stones of mine were quarried near:
By cunning hands were shaped and hewn,
Then carted thus and strait-placed here
To chisel-song and hammer-tune.

And so I bless each passer-by
Who'd trudge for God through sun and rain
To Glendalough: together, I
With Genevieve my Chatelaine.

Specification

Like flame, I'd lantern my poem-chapel
High on a shoulder of Slieve Girkeen, where
She inclines towards Armagh, and syllable
It with wine-stones fresh and craggy featured, each
Rock a face of rosy granite - only
Not nearly so hard, not so geometrically
Unmerciful. Three slim lancets there must
Be, clear-glassed, to slit the apse and stain pink
Dawn-light on the smoothness of the marble
Altar block that guards the sainted well
Encrypted far beneath. Then high upon
The western wall I'd be to pin a window-rose,
Mullioned, its tracery a dream-catcher
Of feathered delicacy to hold and play
The fire-jets of the setting sun: and glazed
With music-panes of blackbird tunes- red, gold,
Blue and olive green : and carpeted the
Purple sanctuary by stillness that flowers
Between two heart-beats of a woman of power.

SET TIMES

Spring Sowing

Walk arm-in-arm with me, my Love, across
The courses of our February haggard,
And we'll watch together Orion, and he to
Be girded with the apron bag of the black

Wind, flinging his crazy scatter of stars
Along the banks of the eastern sky. Oh, and
We'll see too the spring's first crescent
Moon bless the blue slates of our limewashed

Barn in flowing platinum, baptising her
To fulsome womanhood: children again,
We'll hear how within her empty womb,
Once pregnant with seed from a hundred

Harvests, the silence shifts, and gathers
Herself cloud-like into a spinning pillar
Of mystery. And we'll listen to the antique
Half-forgotten hand-turned thresher murmur

Joyously in her sleep, and how, being dug from
Eternity's bed, her lost wheels tremblingly creak,
And in the darkness start once more to whirl in
All the wonderment of a dusty resurrection.

May-fire

Thugamar féin an Samhradh linn
With ourselves have we brought the summer...
(Traditional song welcoming Bealtaine.)

It was half-dreaming of Moses I was that evening, with
Himself in obeisance before a spell-bound bush that
Flared in exodic freedom for the people: and along

A merry deiseal-dance of ritual, deep into the womb of
The greening grove was I led, circling inwards until all
Plumage of sense and logic had moulted from my soul.

Then, just as the last dregs of day were leaching out of the
The western sky, and before the first star had dripped from
The muslin of the heavens, you, the Woman-of-the-Hearth

Who nourished Strangeness of Fire, stepped out.
All evening had I watched you, and then you
Swirled: and as you bent to tend the blaze, the tiny

Sparklets on your dress seemed to catch wild radiance
And become a starfall, and a sheet of mirrored light
Swept up to bathe your womanhood in holy brightness...

There was the man too: he who in quiet wisdom stood before
The gate-of-the-summer blissing all who passed with asperges
Of blossom – scarlet and yellow and green, and a sobbing woman

Near me clutched blue flame to her bosom. When we
Crossed the step, we scattered magic petals on the threshold,
And a bell of thrush-song rang in the throat of the dusk...

SET TIMES

Lá Bealtaine - **May Day**

This was once widely celebrated in Ireland, Scotland and the Isle of Man.

The word Bealtaine itself seems to mean the *Fires of Bel,* Bel being a sun-god beloved for having put the darkness of winter finally to flight, and for leading his people into the warmth of summer, and thus giving hope for a life-giving harvest.

One of the main May-Day rituals involved gathering bunches of seasonal wild flowers on the last day of April, scattering these at window-sills and doorways, and leaving them there overnight.

Deiseal (pronounced desh-al) indicates movement in a clockwise direction as in a procession or a dance.

This turning with the sun was thought to invite good fortune. To progress in an anti-clockwise direction was to attract the opposite.

Midsummer Pilgrimage

Chuaigh mé féin ar mo chois go Cill Shléibhe…
I myself went on foot to Killeavey…
(Traditional song of South Ulster)

A vicious midsummer's it was yon
Year, the rain as wet whips that
Scourged the soaked backs of birthing
Fields -and the constant mists
A-whirl across Slieve Gullion's face
In dense glaucoma wreaths,
Encrusting June-darkened heather with
A sequin shimmer, and squeezing
The whins to dreeping candelabra.

Weak, quaking with gut-hunger,
And kneeling at this lost mountain
Shrine before Moninna's holy well:
The penitential granite cuts hard, biting
Deep as flames of split flint
Into soft knees, and makes me
In this screaming solitude of agony
Forget the Decent Man who squirms,
Pulped, a bloody pinioned
Butterfly upon the splintering cross
Above my head.

Near at hand a flock of clouts
Moored to an ancient bush frenzy and fight

Like demented multi-coloured finches
In the acid wind that from the grey cairn
Of Ballymacdermot pours down its
Spirit-disinfecting draught,
Exploding them to belated gouts
Of cloven fire, that sear the soul
In Pentecostal light and lacerate
Illusion's silken shawl to fluttering pennons.

Midsummer Pilgrimage:
Low on the eastern flank of Slieve Gullion is a shrine dedicated to Saint Moninna of Killeavey, a Celtic Saint, who once ruled as abbess of the nearby convent.
Both the Saint's grave, which is reputed to lie within the modern cemetery, and the shrine itself, are centres for popular pilgrimage.

Cutting the Cailleach
-An Old Man Remembers-
Well, an' have yous put the Cailleach out yet?
Traditional harvest greeting in South Armagh.

Sometimes now, my mind stumbles and swoops, and
I don't know whether today it is, or, have I been
Led to stand upon a flowery bank somewhere on
The blue-green far away of Now-But-Not-Yet? Or
Maybe I'm forever harnessed to the landscape of
A past, where only shadows are my friends. For
Often it seems to me I am but a sorrowful invention
Of my own imagination, my memory rapidly
Unravelling on the cruel knitting needle of the years.

Yet I remember once upon an autumn, and I a boy,
Together with my father's father - the harvest moon a
Muted waterfall of pallid light, climbing, a shy child,
To peep at us from beyond a ridge of Slieve Girkeen -
Our corn all cut, but for the last nine stalks of ancient
Wonderment that bound our people's mythic Queen.

And as though in answer to some strange summons from
Deep within the cavern of the soul, in the softness of that
September dusk, we lined across the pewter of the felled
Field, my bare arms scored to blood: for audience,
The multitude of stooks, head-nodding ghosts. And we,
My grandfather, wisest druid of our race, and I his
Acolyte, all vested with the honeyed twilight, and
Weary from a half-remembered ritual that was long
Since out-of-place. Our sickles drawn by sweating
Hands from scabbards of darkness, were the iron
Flames that would release Her Captive Self.

SET TIMES

So, in ritual turn, as stones skid surfaces of quiet
Pools, we skimmed our blades against the magic stems,
And with the last one's fall, we yelled primordial
Triumph: And in breathless imagination, watched the
Royal train in awesome flight across the meadow,
And its vanishment into labyrinthine hedgerow gloom.

The stalks we fashioned in a wreath of triple-weave,
And in royal memory, named our garland Cailleach.

Cutting the Cailleach:
Cailleach is modern Irish for an old woman, and there is a particular strand of folklore which describes how the spirit of the harvest resides in the last few stalks of corn – in this case, the last stems of oats - left standing in a harvest field.
One tradition would be that these are ceremonially cut by the reapers casting their reaping hooks at them, the fallen stalks being woven into a garland.
An elderly lady in South Armagh once told me that if you looked very carefully, as the cutting occurred, a little old woman clad in a blue gingham apron would always be seen to race from those stalks, and disappear into the hedge!
At least that was the popular belief.
This is as far as the poem goes, but in popular custom the *Cailleach* was afterwards suspended, or otherwise displayed in the farmhouse kitchen, often on top of the dresser.

Autumn Gypsy

One day in last Autumn I laughed at the gaudy spiel of a breeze,
And she to be hawking her raggedy brilliants from window to door,
Screeching aloud from the tree-tops her store
Of garments of scarlet, half green and imperial gold,
Enough that would fill a whole townland of wardrobes and more.

This queen of a breeze I had met for myself at a laneway turn,
Her hair like a gauze of glass stars lighting up the black maw of a ditch.
She asked if I'd buy some clothes from her pack that'd keep me
Sunday resplendent each day o' the week,
But dam all had I got that would buy the tiniest stitch.

Like a blow the shame of my portion struck me that day on the road,
Yet bowing down deep as a Spanish hidalgo I swept off my hat
To show to the lady, who dwelt in the whirlwind,
That though I was poor my blood was noble and rich:
But the chuckle that echoed told me she'd guessed at much more than that.

For she saw through my trickery at once, and enticed me to stop
At playing the fool: a role such as that didn't fit me at all.
So she searched through her satchel of marvels, and
Gave me a heddle all threaded with magical spells.
Weave verses instead, she declared and since then I've followed that call.

Now I long for a woman and she to be veiled in the air,
But linnets keep singing she's far away now a-displaying her pack.
Yet sometimes in autumn or spring when I hear the wild
Yell of the breeze my heart gives a leap in my breast,
And then my soul falls to the hoping that once again she has come back.

SET TIMES

All Souls' Night

Still now the house and smoored
The fire, its fading glow a half-
Remembered cherry frolic upon
A lichened wall. I've swept the

Hearth and in companionable circle
Placed the chairs about the pregnant
Room; for gently now they'll come
A-swirl about me, birling in on steeds

Of misty darkness and riding the
Tenuous wheels of eddying chimney
Draughts. Spectres most benign are
These gracious ghosts of my grey

Ancestors, but I must take my leave
For my kitchen is their court tonight
And I'd not be to stay to overhear
Their whispered discourse of eternity.

All Souls' Night:
Until recently it had been the custom in parts of rural Ulster to sweep the hearth and tidy the kitchen/living-room on the night before All Souls' Day as though in expectation of important visitors.

The general belief was that on that night the spirits of those who had died in the house were permitted to revisit places which had been familiar to them during life.

It was a special time for our distant forebears, since the Celts recognised this period as *Samhain,* their Feast of the Dead, and the beginning of their New Year.

The Christmas

Within myself I yet
Maintain that once I was
The fisherman of Christmas,
Who threw into the still
Pools of frosty solstice
Evenings a net of fields,
And caught within their
Damask mesh a
Whitewashed home, warm
As a womb. Suffused it
Always was with a
Drift of pine-cone smoke
And the scent of paraffin
Oil in chilly bedrooms where
The mandala rays of lamps
Danced glimmering birthday
Jigs with shadows on the
Hillsides of the steeply sloping
Ceilings. Down the stairway
Of the valley the bell of
Carrickcruppen chapel faintly
Rang for the story of wine-rich
Mystery to be whispered in the
Deepest chasm of the darkness.
And with the waning moon
A baby's cry would echo from
The brackened glen beside the
House, decanting from the pagan
Strangeness of the night a melody
That flowed, then melded with
The liquor of the growing light.

SONNETS ON A SPECKLED STONE

43

On Cemetery Sunday

At Carrickcruppen churchyard split a kind

Of cosmic gap, a wide inviting gate

That seemed to me, who watched, to indicate

How we with all our ghosts are close entwined

As woodland roots, that in dark soil confined

Embrace in webs, entangled, intimate

Yet leave each tree a seeming isolate,

As though a singleton each was designed.

With every crystal flake of falling snow

The probing knitwork of the forest jars.

The fugue of all that is its fibres sing

In incandescent chords that breathing show

How midden puddles mirror distant stars,

And Meaning leaps aflame from everything.

Newry Market Recovered

As running boys click sticks on picket rails,

Spun light touched and wrought spells from granite walls.

The Market was a Samarkand where stalls

With banal goods on sale instead bore bales

Of wonder – graips to plant dreams and zinc pails

That brimmed, flowed and frothed with sunshine. Wool shawls

Blazed up, glazed, shot to silk and vendors' calls

Were hoarse birds flying over, scraping trails

Of colour in the raucous air. Then grey

Dusk drummed with farm carts in caravans that

Juddered home like orange flames to small lands

Where unimportance dwells, beyond Cloughrea.

But by each driver's side a stranger sat

And every cart was steered by angel's hands.

Swallows at Carrickbracken

Drunk autumn: greenly deep the drains by lanes

That reel past hazel hedge and laden briar,

Our swallows plot now in the quiet byre

To make escape before September wanes.

For soon they'll fly, each bird, in spiral planes

Above the Church-Rock tower, then onwards, higher,

'Til every throat the sun has dipped in fire,

And the Cailleach Queen herself has blessed the flames.

Then as they wheel, they'll call the summer's soul

To dance with them across Slieve Girkeen's braes -

Away beyond the sky to some lost glen,

Where icy kisses won't be theirs to thole.

But with the passing of the barren days

They'll surely come to grace our byre again.

Swallows at Carrickbracken:
-contains a reference to the *Cailleach*, for which see *Cutting the Cailleach* above.

The Chapel, Hawkstone Hall, Shropshire

– a Summer Idyll-

Sunday morning: and the glistening Hall

Awakes, half dreaming yet of larks that fling

Clear chimes on field and lake, and ring

Like tiny bells from squirrelled woods. They call

Across those gardens, where no hawk can fall

To wound, or cause dishevelment to wincing wing:

For in that spot all voices choir to sing

The spirit whole again, and hearts enthral

With loveliness. Aglow with dawn and grace

The chapel organ softly tones, then folds

In holy chord and cadence all who'd kneel in prayer

And worship in that incense-clouded place,

As once again the chaliced Tale is told,

How Christ will come this day to visit there.

Benburb Priory

Caught on an age-hewn summit of the fabulous steeps

The Priory soars above the thundering weir,

Where beds Blackwater's darkly roaring deeps,

And wild redemptive music echoes clear.

And through the wide flung-open Servite gates have passed

A multitude soul-wounded from our mythic fray,

Found ancient solace here, and at the last

Arose once more, and walked serene away.

Then in this green and god-enchanted place I would beseech

The Spirit of passion to enter me anew,

Her seven-fold lesson of profound simplicity to teach,

Yet leave my senses drenched in Easter dew

- As in the garden stillness of the Priory grounds

The Lady walks again at Vesper-time - all sable-gowned.

Benburb Priory:
This is a house of the medieval Servite Order. The Friars of Benburb have made a significant contribution to the spiritual, social and cultural fabric of Northern Ireland since they became officially established there in 1949.
Traditionally the Servites venerate the Blessed Virgin in her role as Mother of Sorrows.
A legend describes how Our Lady appeared to the Founding Brethren, and gifted them with a black habit, hence the reference in the poem to the sable-clad Lady.

RANDOM GATHERINGS

49

Presents

Had I a gift to gift us with
I'd give us a spectrum broad,
Then the world we'd see would be coloured
As it birthed from the womb of God.

Plain black and white would be banished
To the coils of some sunless maze,
Then only the tints that life had mixed
Would set the world ablaze.

For life is a complex beauty,
For all it harbours a flaw,
Yet some would seek to contain it,
By quoting from texts of law -

Oh, and using long words to impress us,
They would sell us their souls' intent
And so earnestly would they ply them,
One would think that they knew what they meant!

For such folk speak not out of wisdom,
As they strive to control us by might
And thus again Christus is hanging
'Twixt thieves of black and white.

Passion-tide

You brought your child to church last night, Ma'am,
- A precious scrap that one night's passion-tide had
Cast upon your shore, and in the chapel porch you

Left the wheelchair. Right clumsily you carried her
To your seat, her purple velvet dress rucked up
To show thin legs in wee white tights a-dangle,

Twisted and threshing like storm-torn winter
Twigs. Aye, a brave lump she was, and she to be
Ten years old. All during Mass you sat, her bobbling

Head empillowed on your shoulder, her childish
Crowing was a frightened curlew cry that probed
And questioned the sterile dignity of our staid devotion.

But a sort of ripple it was too, that splashed
And tinted us with all the common colours
Of humanity. You took communion, you and

Your girl-child, and then you held a plastic water
Bottle to her quivering lips and lulled her into stillness.
I wonder if on that night some strange and tortured

Prophet had passed amongst us, and did I mistake
The wounded bird-like calling of your child
For the primal roar of mighty Sinai's thundering?

The Sacrament of the Scarf

Once at a Mass,
Like cut flesh bruised,
My spirit oozed forth
Trickles of raw pain.
Then late a woman came,
A dowdy granny grey
In costume creased
Faded and dulled.
Yet on her head she
Wore a Botticelli Roma scarf
Aglow with a thousand
Shining fancies -a laughing
Latin glory of a scarf.
For a sign of peace she
Turned right round and
Proffered me a grubby hand.
God bless you Love,
She murmured, and
For the pain of the healing
I almost cried.

A Merchant Prince

-for my mother who remembered Felim -

Regular as the sunrise, and just as welcome,
With basket full of gaudy trifles a-swing upon your
Arm, you used to call with us, a tatterdemalion
Merchant-wanderer with strange news-bulletins

From deep in the far-off land of your simplicity.
Sure of your tea-and-soda-farl welcome, my mother
Always seated you with honour at our kitchen
Table, where, for once the centre of respect, in

Crippled tongue you offered garbled thanks. But
Yet, in jest, behind parental backs, we sometimes bade
You pray: *Go on Faily! Say your prayers! Say your
Prayers for us!* Then, you'd stand, and in a parody of

Solemn ritual you'd throw your torn cap aside revealing
Thus the sad misshapenness of a skull too-large. And
Casting dulled eyes toward heaven you'd utter fountains
Of hoarse prayer in a Doric all your own. But one day

You ceased to come, and only now do I realise how
Much you'd meant to me: for I remember how in the
Vacuity of your smiling, I had sometimes seen reflected
A fleeting shadow of the sublime stupidity of Christ.

Mucky *Pieta*

No flawless marble sculpture this: when first I saw him
From the safety of my car, full foetus-like he was, curled up
In sleep amid the chaos of the reeking weeds. Yet was there
Also something child-like in his frailty. And faintly comical

Too, I thought – uncomfortably indeed– for the emptied
Vodka flask that lay beside his fallen cap seemed to have
Another kind of tale to tell. Beneath his slobbering mouth
A mound of vomit steamed… Then from out behind the

Falling curtain of the twilit rain a Woman stepped–
Whether daughter, wife or lover –or just a friend– but
Kneeling down in mud she drew a tissue from her bag,
And having wiped his lips she stooped and gently kissed

His balding brow. With difficulty then she hoisted up his head
Upon her ample thighs and held him thus. And all unconsciously
She built a shrine that housed a holy tableau carved from flesh.
I found it quite bewildering to see *Pieta* in the street.

Welcome the Singer
After the Irish of Blind Séamas MacCuarta C.1650 -1733

Hail that bird whose voice of glory

Haunts this wood from a hawthorn bough.

Though I cannot read the Springtime story,

Rejoicing I listen in wonderment how

The spring-bird's song rings the woodland core. She

Beckons the summer with every note,

And as Ireland glistens with flowers the more she

Scatters their name from tremulous throat

Like droplets of salve that would endow

With light these eyes that darkness smote:

Through the mist in the forest now

I hear the chimes of the cuckoo float.

Great sorrow it is that blindness should be my fate,

And my not greeting Summer who enters in right royal state

To liven good people with tidings that celebrate

Their loving and living, and brightness and light create.

Imagination

Unstop the flask! Uncap the spring,
And let imagination spill
Across the world to soak its soul,
And dried up dykes of logic fill!

Then let it bathe long-blinkered eyes
And free folk walled in Caution's tower!
To saturate the fields of heart
Upend the cask! Unleash its power!

With streams of beauty swell its flood,
Until its tides in brightness flare
To light the land and penetrate
Minds starched in greyness everywhere.

Vendor

Deep in the market-place of heart
Alone I stand to chant my wares,
As up and down good people pass
With blank unseeing stares.

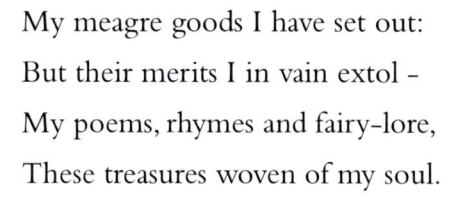

My meagre goods I have set out:
But their merits I in vain extol –
My poems, rhymes and fairy-lore,
These treasures woven of my soul.

So won't you buy these lovely things,
My olden songs and new.
Yet even should you still pass by,
May blessings go with you.

European Union

Hunched in a draughty entry off the High Street,
His fussy hands, brown and stubby as sparrow-flutter,
Flicker across the keys of an antique accordion.

So I stop to listen, watching the lean swarthiness
Of his foreign-seeming face, loose-jawed, exotic,
His eyes half-closed in music-daze. The notes the

Cunning fingers weave from out the wheezing
Bellows loom are the goldfinch charms of
Fur Elise, as they soar and dive, chasing each

Other through the bustling shopping crowds. Then
Into the chalice of the plastic cup which holds his
Artiste-stipend I place my tribute, hoping the heart

Of his Elise in far-off Bucharest will quicken to a
Melody made for her in Belfast. I somehow think
That Beethoven would have approved.

Love-song

Bored out of my tree I sat daily beside you,
Enduring your endless interrogation:
Where do you live now? repeated corncrake-fashion
Over again - and over.
Then would come a pause, until once more you ask:
Where do you live now?
My heart is broken as I look at you,
Your grey eyes glazed as shards of dull china,
Flecked with blood.
But I meet your empty gaze and watch
Your thin blue-veined fingers
Gently stroke the fringe of the tartan rug
About your knees.
One day my branch broke and I toppled into reality,
And I realised
That although you may have echoed
Where do you live now?
You were instead saying to me
Over again - and over:
I love you.

Lucy

I met in the heroic bouquet of
Lusaka market a tiny ragdoll
Woman, gap toothed, and dusty, swathed in blue-
Checked wrap-a-round - one webbish hand outstretched
To capture chance, the other resting

On the shoulder of a boy - her staff and
Guide. Today I see her eyes, deep grottoes,
Dark and lustrous, pink rimmed: each a heaving
Pool of shining flies fatt'ning on the pus
They find there… *Please give,* she importunes,

Please give! And then she stamps my soul with wounds,
Inflamed and rancid from our encounter,
That smart and fester sometimes in the thickness
Of my nights and make me plead in turn:
Won't you go away…? Only go away…

Pick-Pocket

"And he said to her, 'Daughter, your faith has made you well...'" (Mk 5:34)

Only a tiny shimmer of a thing...and her fading

Womanhood a-leaching slow away in streams

Of red fragility...she tried to wear her

Self-embarrassment beneath a torn veil of

Dignity...for she was shadow-light...white

As a wisp of sheep's wool you'd see rippling

On a thorn-bush on a March day... yet she

Had courage – and a sense of time forbye

...for on the instant, and she, but a seeming

Cipher on the thistled edge of a boiling crowd

Dared all unseen – to touch the trailing edge

Of Pity's dusty coat, and from the Mystery of

Of its cosmic pocket...filch forth her healing.

Trout

I know a well, a brooding pool of
Bubbled starriness, that sounds
Dark echoes in the hazled angle

Of a twilit field. Deep within
The silent chords of water swims
A sacred trout, a single harp all strung

With gold and stippled pink, that plucks
Forever music flecked from lost and
Long-drowned walls of ancient

Memory. My father told how peace-
Of-soul would always be the lot of
Those who lingered here to drink.

Pilgrims

Separate travellers you and I, who

Through some great mystery, as Folk of God,

Together occupy this little time and space.

Except for our humanity, and the Blood Royale

Which proves us kin, as strangers in the

Darkness we may be. And yet, since

Pilgrimage is Lenten fare indeed without

Companion, after the manner of those

Who'd walk in step, may I embreak with

You the bread of my experience? Then,

In my doing thus, mayhap you'd honour

Me by pouring forth your story's wine:

For of pilgrim stock are you and I, and

Just as certainly, by holy pathways led.

NOTES